SCHOLASTIC

OVERHEAD WRITING LESSONS

EXCEPTIONAL ESSAYS

by Carol Rawlings Miller
and Sarah Glasscock

NEW YORK • TORONTO • LONDON • AUCKLAND • SYDNEY
MEXICO CITY • NEW DELHI • HONG KONG • BUENOS AIRES

Teaching Resources

This book is dedicated to Jack.

—CRM

AcKnowledgments

Sincerest thanks are due to Jeanne and Milton Miller and Charles and Joan Rawlings, for being devoted, babysitting grandparents, and to my husband James Miller, for patience.

More than one editor made this series possible. I really am indebted to Ellen Ungaro—not only for her expertise and encouragement, but for her sense of humor. I also wish to thank Virginia Dooley; she has been, amongst other things, patient. And to Wendy Murray, for weighing in helpfully, many thanks.

—CRM

Cover Design by Josué Castilleja
Cover Illustration by Eric Brace
Interior Design by Brian LaRossa

Book ISBN 0-439-56816-1
Product ISBN 0-439-22258-3

Printed in the U.S.A.

4 5 6 7 8 9 10 40 12 11 10 09 08 07

Contents

Introduction

Writing is a complex task that requires students to integrate many skills all at once. The complexity of writing and the importance of basic mastery puts pressure on teachers and students alike. In this book, we've tried to break down the process of writing an essay. The activities and exercises in these pages help build a strong foundation through reading and analyzing essays and by taking students through the steps of writing an essay.

The Approach of This Book

This book addresses the following aspects of essays:

- structure
- types (expository, narrative, descriptive, persuasive)
- brainstorming
- writing a thesis
- outlining and taking notes
- writing the introduction, body, and conclusion
- introducing transitions
- editing and proofreading

We suggest that you teach the lessons in sequence, as the lessons build upon each other.

An overhead transparency accompanies most of the lessons in this book. The transparencies give a brief overview and present examples for the class to analyze together. Each lesson also includes at least one reproducible that provides students with more practice and/or reference sheets. When a lesson includes an overhead, we suggest that you display it for reference as students work on the reproducible.

The teaching pages display the pertinent National Language Arts Standards as well as information about how to present the overheads and the reproducibles. Writing Practice is a feature that allows students to apply the lesson skills in their own writing. Some lessons also include sections on Enriching the Lesson and Teaching Tips.

On Overhead Writing Lessons

Strong Sentences, *Powerful Paragraphs*, and *Exceptional Essays* comprise the Overhead Writing Lessons series of books. Each book targets and teaches specific grammar and writing skills that will make your students better and more confident writers.

Exceptional Essays

◆ Purpose ◆

To give an overview of the elements of an essay

In writing essays, students integrate all the skills they've learned about sentences and paragraphs into one piece of writing. Very simply put, in an essay, a writer explains what he or she thinks and why. To write exceptional essays, students must successfully combine form and content to express their points of view. This lesson begins the process by giving an overview of the essay and its structure.

National Language Arts Standards:

- ▲ Evaluates own and others' writing
- ▲ Uses reading skills and strategies to understand a variety of informational texts

▲ Launching Activity: Exceptional Essays (Overhead 1)

Read aloud "This Movie Is Full of Holes." Then ask students about their opinions on other books that have been made into movies, such as the Harry Potter series. Be quick to question students who offer vague statements to help them articulate the reasons behind their opinions. Bring the discussion to a close by explaining that they've presented good ideas for some potentially exceptional essays. Go over the definition of an essay and information on the overhead. Tell students that an essay is usually three paragraphs or longer, and that the sentences and paragraphs in an essay work together to make an important point.

Reiterate that there are different types of essays, but that all essays share the same format: introduction, thesis, body, and conclusion.

Have students reread the essay on the overhead independently. Then discuss the questions at the bottom of the overhead. For question 1, remind students that the thesis always appears in the first paragraph, the introduction. They're looking for one or two sentences that tell the reader what the essay is about. Underline or highlight the thesis in the essay: *But kids who really loved reading the book Holes by Louis Sachar will also love the movie*. Be sure students understand that the thesis isn't always the first sentence of an essay.

Then bracket the second and third paragraphs, and explain that this is the body of the essay because it contains details that support the thesis. After students point out the facts discussed in the body—acting and writing—ask: ***Do you notice that the writer briefly mentions acting and writing in the introduction?*** Allow students to express their opinions freely about the effectiveness of the conclusion. Keep the discussion centered on the writer's success or failure at proving his or her point rather than their own personal feelings about the book and movie.

Overhead Transparency

- ◆ Exceptional Essays

Reproducible

- ◆ An Exceptional Essay

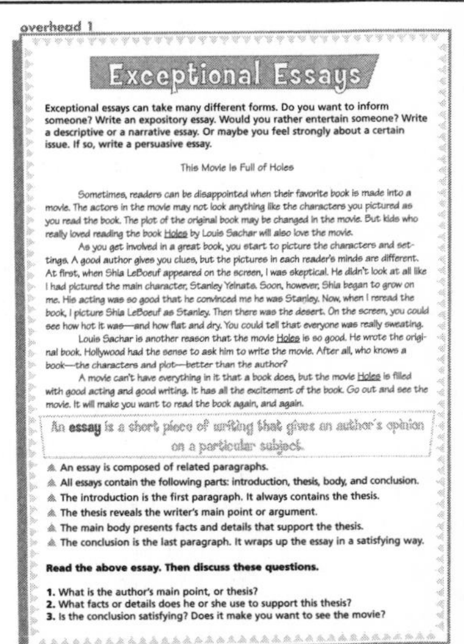

overhead 1

Exceptional Essays

Exceptional essays can take many different forms. Do you want to inform someone? Write an expository essay. Would you rather entertain someone? Write a descriptive or a narrative essay. Or maybe you feel strongly about a certain issue. If so, write a persuasive essay.

This Movie Is Full of Holes

Sometimes, readers can be disappointed when their favorite book is made into a movie. The actors in the movie may not look anything like the characters you pictured as you read the book. The plot of the original book may be changed in the movie. But kids who really loved reading the book Holes by Louis Sachar will also love the movie.

As you get involved in a great book, you start to picture the characters and settings. A good author gives you clues, but the pictures in each reader's minds are different. At first, when Shia LeBoeuf appeared on the screen, I was skeptical. He didn't look at all like I had pictured the main character, Stanley Yelnats. Soon, however, Shia began to grow on me. His acting was so good that he convinced me he was Stanley. Now, when I reread the book, I picture Shia LeBoeuf as Stanley. Then there was the desert. On the screen, you could see how hot it was—and how flat and dry. You could tell that everyone was really sweating.

Louis Sachar is another reason that the movie Holes is so good. He wrote the original book. Hollywood had the sense to ask him to write the movie. After all, who knows a book—the characters and plot—better than the author?

A movie can't have everything in it that a book does, but the movie Holes is filled with good acting and good writing. It has all the excitement of the book. Go out and see the movie. It will make you want to read the book again, and again.

An **essay** is a short piece of writing that gives an author's opinion on a particular subject.

- ▲ An essay is composed of related paragraphs.
- ▲ All essays contain the following parts: introduction, thesis, body, and conclusion.
- ▲ The introduction is the first paragraph. It always contains the thesis.
- ▲ The thesis reveals the writer's main point or argument.
- ▲ The main body presents facts and details that support the thesis.
- ▲ The conclusion is the last paragraph. It wraps up the essay in a satisfying way.

Read the above essay. Then discuss these questions.

1. What is the author's main point, or thesis?
2. What facts or details does he or she use to support this thesis?
3. Is the conclusion satisfying? Does it make you want to see the movie?

Student Reproducible

An Exceptional Essay: After reading aloud "Acoma, the City in the Sky," review the parts of the essay. Then give students time to read it on their own. Explain that it is an expository essay. The writer presents facts about a topic. Then discuss the facts students noticed in the essay. You may want to model your own response first: One of the first facts I noticed was that Acoma sits on a 367-foot-tall mesa. When a writer gives such a specific detail, I'm pretty certain that he or she has done some research to find that information. Giving the names of people and places, dates, and measurements is a good way to present facts. Then ask students to circle, underline, or highlight other facts in the essay.

Writing Practice

Challenge students to put their opinions into essay form. Have them write their own reviews about a movie based on a book. Do they think the transfer from page to screen was a success or a failure? What evidence do they have to support their opinion? At this early stage, it's important for students to get their opinions down on paper. The goal here is to get students writing.

Teaching Tip

Select a variety of expository, narrative, descriptive, and persuasive essays for students to read as you use this book in your classroom. You might store them in labeled envelopes, folders, or boxes. The structures of the essays are the same, but the differences in the writers' voices, tones, opinions, and feelings will open up the world of essays for students.

Name ______________________ Date ______________

An Exceptional Essay

Acoma, the City in the Sky

introduction [The Acoma [AH-koh-mah] Pueblo, one of the 19 Indian Pueblos in New Mexico, sits on top of a 367-foot-high sandstone mesa. Because of its location, Acoma is known as the Sky City. Location is also the reason that the Acoma Pueblo is considered to be the oldest inhabited village in the United States. It has beautiful, 360-degree views. Acoma was easy to defend—until the Spanish arrived.]

thesis

body [The first white men visited Acoma in 1540. Searching for gold, Francisco Vasquez de Coronado and his Spanish expedition stopped at Acoma. Pedro de Castaneda, a member of the expedition, wrote, "The village was very strong because it was up on a rock out of reach, having steep sides in every direction. . . . There was a wall of large and small stones at the top, which they could roll down without showing themselves, so that no army could possibly be strong enough to capture the village."

In 1598, the Acoma people met another Spaniard. Juan de Oñate had declared himself governor of the Pueblo lands. He demanded that the Indians swear obedience to Spain. Soon the Pueblos and Spaniards were fighting. When Oñate's nephew was killed at Acoma, things took a turn for the worse.

Oñate sent soldiers to Acoma in the winter of 1599. From the top of the mesa, the Acoma people threw ice, spears, stones, and arrows at their enemy. Then the Spanish sounded their trumpets to signal an attack. While the Acoma people defended the trail at the top of the mesa, the Spanish climbed the mesa's steep walls on another, undefended side. The village was destroyed. The Acoma people were enslaved by the Spanish.

But slowly, the people escaped and returned to Acoma to rebuild their homes. Although the village doesn't have electricity or running water, families continue to live there today. A road was built to the top of the mesa in 1929, so the villagers don't have to carry water up the steep trail as they did before.]

conclusion [To reach Acoma today, visitors can climb the trail or ride a bus to the top. They can see the smoke stains on the southwest side of the mesa that were caused by the Spanish cannons. They can stare up the mesa and wonder how the heavily armed soldiers managed to climb its sheer sides. But, at the top, gazing at Enchanted Mesa across the valley, visitors will also understand why the Acoma people continue to live in the Sky City.]

The Expository Essay

National Language Arts Standards:

- Writes expository compositions
- Identifies and stays on topic
- Establishes coherence within paragraphs

◆ Purpose ◆

To recognize the elements of an expository essay

During their school careers, students will probably be asked to write expository essays more than any other type of essay. To successfully do this, they must be able to tell the difference between a fact and an opinion. And they must also weigh which facts to use to support their thesis. We are also helping students strengthen their research skills when they write expository essays.

Overhead Transparency

- Types of Essays

Reproducible

- An Expository Essay

Launching Activity: Types of Essays (Overhead 2)

Before you display this overhead, hand out copies of the expository essay, "From Andrea to Wendy: How Hurricanes Get Their Names" (page 9). Read aloud the essay, and discuss the content briefly with students. Point out that, like all essays, it has an introduction, thesis, body, and conclusion. Then pose questions such as the following: *Can you tell what the writer thinks about hurricanes from this essay? Does the writer use facts or opinions in this essay?*

Introduce the information on the overhead, and be sure students understand that this essay is based on fact. Model how the title and body of the essay relates to the thesis: I know from the title and the body that this essay is about how and why hurricanes are named. The second and third sentences in the introduction explain that to me. Remember that a thesis can be more than one sentence, and it can occur anywhere in the introduction.

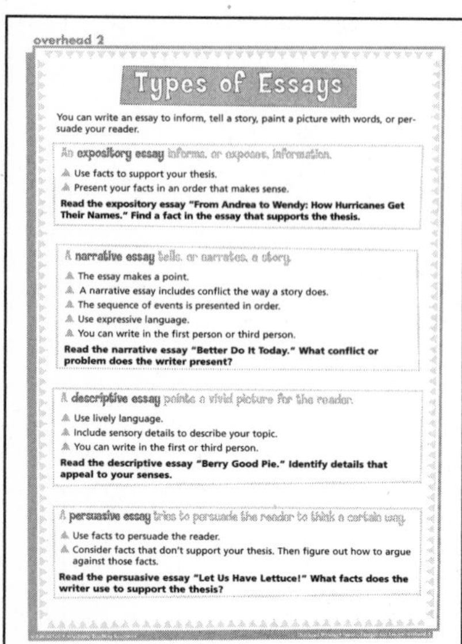

overhead 2

Types of Essays

You can write an essay to inform, tell a story, paint a picture with words, or persuade your reader.

An **expository essay** informs, or exposes, information.

- Use facts to support your thesis.
- Present your facts in an order that makes sense.

Read the expository essay "From Andrea to Wendy: How Hurricanes Get Their Names." Find a fact in the essay that supports the thesis.

A **narrative essay** tells, or narrates, a story.

- The essay makes a point.
- A narrative essay includes conflict the way a story does.
- The sequence of events is presented in order.
- Use expressive language.
- You can write in the first person or third person.

Read the narrative essay "Better Do It Today." What conflict or problem does the writer present?

A **descriptive essay** paints a vivid picture for the reader.

- Use lively language.
- Include sensory details to describe your topic.
- You can write in the first or third person.

Read the descriptive essay "Berry Good Pie." Identify details that appeal to your senses.

A **persuasive essay** tries to persuade the reader to think a certain way.

- Use facts to persuade the reader.
- Consider facts that don't support your thesis. Then figure out how to argue against those facts.

Read the persuasive essay "Let Us Have Lettuce!" What facts does the writer use to support the thesis?

Student Reproducible

An Expository Essay: From Andrea to Wendy: How Hurricanes Get Their Names: After completing the overhead activity, ask students to read this essay independently. Then have them highlight, underline, or circle all the facts that support the thesis.

Writing Practice

Ask students to write a three-paragraph expository essay. They should be familiar enough with the topic so they won't have to do any research. The idea here is to get students writing. Suggested prompts: What are the similarities and differences between being in the first grade and being in the (students' grade)? Why should a tourist visit our town or city?

Name ______________________ Date ______________

An Expository Essay

From Andrea to Wendy: How Hurricanes Get Their Names

introduction [In 2004, several hurricanes were brewing in the Atlantic Ocean. Thanks to the system of naming hurricanes, meteorologists and the public were able to tell the storms apart. That system of naming hurricanes has changed over the years. But if a hurricane is never named after you, don't be surprised. With very few changes, the list is recycled every six years.]

thesis

body [People have been naming hurricanes for hundreds of years. Hurricanes in the West Indies were the first to receive names. The storms were named for the saint's day on which they occurred. For instance, the first hurricane San Felipe struck Puerto Rico on September 13, 1876, and the second hurricane San Felipe struck the island on September 13, 1928. Then Australian meteorologist, Clement Wragge, began giving women's names to hurricanes in the late 1800s. The use of women's names became official in this country when the United States National Weather Service adopted the idea in 1953. The system changed again in 1979 when both men's and women's names appeared on the list of hurricane names.

The World Meteorological Organization has created a list of names for hurricanes in the Atlantic Ocean. Every six years, the names are repeated. For example, the first four names on the list for 1998 and 2004 were Alex, Bonnie, Charley, and Danielle. The lists are alphabetical, but they don't include the letters Q, U, X, Y, or Z. The names may be French, Spanish, or English because those are the major languages in the area. Once a storm reaches a wind speed of 39 miles per hour, it is given a name. And if a storm causes severe damage, its name may be retired and never used again.]

conclusion [As of October 2004, fourteen hurricanes in the Atlantic Ocean had been given names. Without these names, it might have been difficult for us to distinguish between some of these storms. Several of them—Charley, Frances, Jeanne, and Ivan—caused severe damage. In fact, President Bush asked Congress for $12.2 billion dollars in aid. Have we heard the last of Hurricane Charley or Frances? Will the name of one or more of these destructive 2004 hurricanes be retired?]

The Narrative Essay

National Language Arts Standards:

- Writes narrative accounts
- Identifies and stays on topic
- Establishes coherence within paragraphs

◆ Purpose ◆

To recognize the elements of a narrative essay

Sometimes, writing a narrative essay can seem deceptively simple: You tell a story about something or someone. But a narrative essay is more than a stream-of-consciousness exercise. It must have shape and structure, conflict and resolution. Students always have plenty of stories to tell, but their narrative essays can often fail to make a point or teach a lesson.

Overhead Transparency

- Types of Essays

Reproducible

- A Narrative Essay

Launching Activity: Types of Essays (Overhead 2)

Go over the information about narrative essays on the overhead. Then read aloud "Better Do It Today" (page 11) or call on a volunteer to do so. After discussing the content of the essay, point out that it's written in the first person, which makes it seem more personal. Then pose the following questions: *Who do you think the narrator or person telling the story is? What point is the writer trying to make?*

What students should notice about this essay is its more informal, storytelling style. Then ask them to read the essay independently and identify the narrator's conflict.

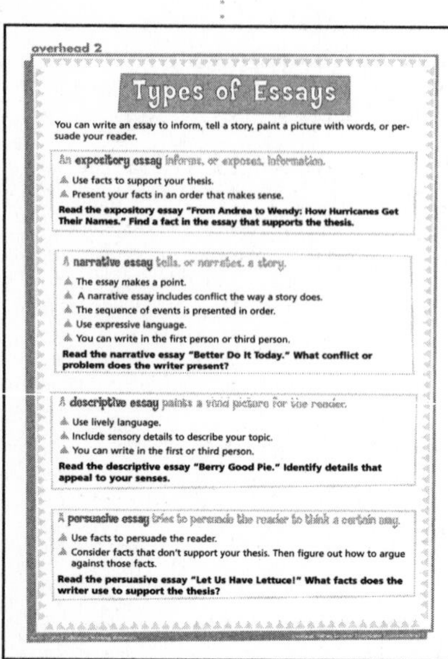

overhead 2

Types of Essays

You can write an essay to inform, tell a story, paint a picture with words, or persuade your reader.

An **expository essay** informs, or exposes, information.

- Use facts to support your thesis.
- Present your facts in an order that makes sense.

Read the expository essay "From Andrea to Wendy: How Hurricanes Get Their Names." Find a fact in the essay that supports the thesis.

A **narrative essay** tells, or narrates, a story.

- The essay makes a point.
- A narrative essay includes conflict the way a story does.
- The sequence of events is presented in order.
- Use expressive language.
- You can write in the first person or third person.

Read the narrative essay "Better Do It Today." What conflict or problem does the writer present?

A **descriptive essay** paints a vivid picture for the reader.

- Use lively language.
- Include sensory details to describe your topic.
- You can write in the first or third person.

Read the descriptive essay "Berry Good Pie." Identify details that appeal to your senses.

A **persuasive essay** tries to persuade the reader to think a certain way.

- Use facts to persuade the reader.
- Consider facts that don't support your thesis. Then figure out how to argue against those facts.

Read the persuasive essay "Let Us Have Lettuce!" What facts does the writer use to support the thesis?

Student Reproducible

A Narrative Essay: After the overhead activity, encourage students to write a brief summary of the essay on the back of the reproducible. Then ask them to highlight, circle, or underline the language in the essay that they think is particularly expressive. Challenge students to select one particular word or phrase and articulate what makes it lively and fresh.

Writing Practice

Have students write a narrative essay of at least three paragraphs. Suggested prompts: What lesson did you learn on the best day in your life? What lesson did you learn on one of the worst day in your life?

Name ______________________________ Date ____________________

A Narrative Essay

Better Do It Today

introduction [Our parents are in charge of raising us, and that's a big job. They're supposed to tell us how and why to do things—and we're supposed to listen. Then you reach the age of twelve or so. Your parents' lessons start sounding something like, "Blah, blah, blah, blah." Sometimes, you tune them out. You think you know better.
thesis Well, let me tell you a story that may get you to perk up your ears the next time your parents tell you to do something.]

body [I had a paper due on Monday. On Friday, after school, my mom said, "How's that essay on roller coasters going? I'm going to the library in case you want to come along and do some more research." Some more research? I hadn't even started researching! I also know my mom pretty well. She knew I hadn't even started the paper. That was her way of nudging me to get going on it.

The next morning, she nudged me a little harder. In fact, Mom nudged me awake at seven in the morning—on a Saturday! "Better get that paper done today," she warned me. "Remember, we're going to Gigi's on Sunday." (Gigi is my grandmother. She's a great grandmother.) I pulled the pillow over my face and went back to sleep. I dreamed I was on the world's tallest roller coaster. It kept dropping and dropping and never reached the bottom. That and the phone got me out of bed.

My best friend, M.P., wanted me to help her walk her neighbor's dogs. Luckily, Dad had forgotten about the roller-coaster paper, too, and said I could go. No wonder M.P. wanted my help: She was walking all of her neighbors' dogs. Then we had to give them all baths. I dragged home that afternoon with a very sore arm and wet hair. Dad tried to perk me up by reliving some of his best roller-coaster rides for me. "You'd better get that paper done tonight," he warned. "Because, blah, blah, blah." I got as far as printing out some information about the world's tallest, longest, fastest, and oldest roller coasters before I fell asleep.

To make a long story short, Dad and I stayed home on Sunday so I could work on my paper. Mom went to Gigi's and had a terrific time. You know what they did? They went to the amusement park and spent all day riding the Super Twister Coaster. That was supposed to be my surprise for finishing my paper in time.]

conclusion [I learned my lesson. Now, when my parents say, "You'd better do it today," I do. Not only do I get the job done in time, but I also know there's going to be a surprise waiting for me.]

The Descriptive Essay

National Language Arts Standards:

- Writes expressive compositions
- Identifies and stays on topic
- Establishes coherence within paragraphs

Overhead Transparency

- Types of Essays

Reproducible

- A Descriptive Essay

Purpose

To recognize the elements of a descriptive essay

Writing a descriptive essay challenges students to expand their vocabulary and to use all their senses to see things in new ways. When students have an understanding of the structure and process of writing an essay, they'll have more confidence in exploring language and taking chances in expressing themselves.

Launching Activity: Types of Essays (Overhead 2)

Distribute copies of "Berry Good Pie" (page 13) to students. The aim of this descriptive essay is to make students wish they had a slice of that raspberry pie.

After reading aloud the essay, talk about the images and thoughts that came to students as you read. Then present the information about narrative essays on the overhead. Guide students in discovering the sensory images the writer uses. For instance, you may talk about your favorite image: *My favorite part of a pie is the crust. It has to be light and flaky. It shouldn't be tough. As I read, I almost felt as if I could taste the layers of buttery crust melting in my mouth.*

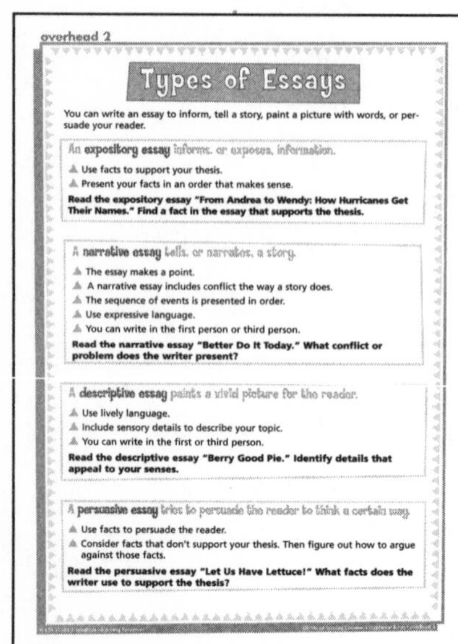

overhead 2

Types of Essays

You can write an essay to inform, tell a story, paint a picture with words, or persuade your reader.

An **expository essay** informs, or exposes, information.

- Use facts to support your thesis.
- Present your facts in an order that makes sense.

Read the expository essay "From Andrea to Wendy: How Hurricanes Get Their Names." Find a fact in the essay that supports the thesis.

A **narrative essay** tells, or narrates, a story.

- The essay makes a point.
- A narrative essay includes conflict the way a story does.
- The sequence of events is presented in order.
- Use expressive language.
- You can write in the first person or third person.

Read the narrative essay "Better Do It Today." What conflict or problem does the writer present?

A **descriptive essay** paints a vivid picture for the reader.

- Use lively language.
- Include sensory details to describe your topic.
- You can write in the first or third person.

Read the descriptive essay "Berry Good Pie." Identify details that appeal to your senses.

A **persuasive essay** tries to persuade the reader to think a certain way.

- Use facts to persuade the reader.
- Consider facts that don't support your thesis. Then figure out how to argue against those facts.

Read the persuasive essay "Let Us Have Lettuce!" What facts does the writer use to support the thesis?

Student Reproducible

A Descriptive Essay: Berry Good Pie: Challenge students to name details in the essay and to identify which of their senses each one appeals to. Then have them mark the words, phrases, and sentences that create a vivid picture of the pie in their minds.

Writing Practice

Tell students to write a descriptive essay that contains at least three paragraphs. Suggested prompts: How do you feel on a hot summer day (or a cold winter day)? How would you describe a member of your family or a friend so that a stranger would be able to picture him or her?

Name ______________________________ Date ______________________

A Descriptive Essay

Berry Good Pie

introduction [Nobody makes a pie that has a more delicious, oozing filling or a flakier
thesis crust than my grandfather. That's right, my grandfather, Josh. My grandmother, Hazel, can't roll out a tender pie crust to save her life, but her husband can produce four of the sweetest, spiciest, juiciest, bursting-with-flavor raspberry pies in about an hour. The scent of summer bursts out of the oven when those pies are baking.]

body [As you may have guessed, my grandfather's specialty pie is raspberry pie. He always uses the very best berries. He knows they're the best because he grows the berries himself. The freezer in my grandparents' house is filled with sealed bags of berries, so we can have raspberry pie even in the deep cold of winter. And here is Josh's secret: He adds a little squeeze of lemon juice and a grating of ginger to his berry filling. The lemon gives the pie a zing and keeps it from being too sweet. The ginger gives it mystery. You sit back and wonder: Hmmm, what is that taste?

Josh's mother taught him how to make pies. He says the secret of a tender crust is to keep everything as cold as can be—the butter he cuts into chunks; the water that moistens the flour, salt, butter, and touch of sugar; and the bowl and utensils. My great-grandmother's pie specialty was pecan pies. She won over 40 pie contests in her life! Who would be a better teacher than an award-winning cook?]

conclusion [Years of experience, homegrown berries, a zingy and mysterious filling, and cold pie dough make Josh Warner's raspberry pie the best in the world. If my words don't convince you, then one bite certainly would.]

The Persuasive Essay

National Language Arts Standards:

- Writes persuasive compositions
- Identifies and stays on topic
- Establishes coherence within paragraphs

◆ Purpose ◆

To recognize the elements of a persuasive essay

It takes more than a passionate opinion about a topic to influence another person. Persuasive essays begin with a thesis that presents an argument. Then the writer must rely on facts to sway his or her reader. To have a solid grasp of what a persuasive essay is, and how powerful it can be, students must be able to differentiate between fact and opinion.

Overhead Transparency

- Types of Essays

Reproducible

- A Persuasive Essay

Launching Activity: Types of Essays (Overhead 2)

After students read "Let Us Have Lettuce!" independently, call on a volunteer to read it aloud. Then talk about the writer's opinion about cafeteria food and vending machines in schools. How does your own school handle food choices for students? What changes, if any, should the school make? Then share the information on the overhead with students. Challenge students to identify the facts the writer uses to make his or her argument.

Go over each part of the essay, and reinforce the idea that all essays have the same structure. Take a few minutes to have students compare and contrast all four essays (pages 9, 11, 13, 15).

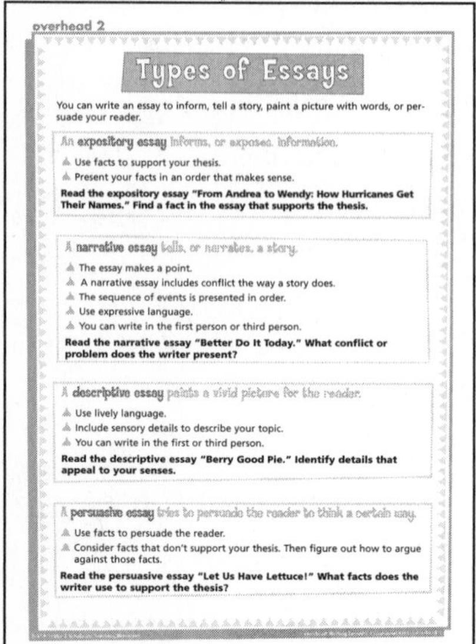

overhead 2

Types of Essays

You can write an essay to inform, tell a story, paint a picture with words, or persuade your reader.

An **expository essay** informs, or exposes, information.

- Use facts to support your thesis.
- Present your facts in an order that makes sense.

Read the expository essay "From Andrea to Wendy: How Hurricanes Get Their Names." Find a fact in the essay that supports the thesis.

A **narrative essay** tells, or narrates, a story.

- The essay makes a point.
- A narrative essay includes conflict the way a story does.
- The sequence of events is presented in order.
- Use expressive language.
- You can write in the first person or third person.

Read the narrative essay "Better Do It Today." What conflict or problem does the writer present?

A **descriptive essay** paints a vivid picture for the reader.

- Use lively language.
- Include sensory details to describe your topic.
- You can write in the first or third person.

Read the descriptive essay "Berry Good Pie." Identify details that appeal to your senses.

A **persuasive essay** tries to persuade the reader to think a certain way.

- Use facts to persuade the reader.
- Consider facts that don't support your thesis. Then figure out how to argue against those facts.

Read the persuasive essay "Let Us Have Lettuce!" What facts does the writer use to support the thesis?

Student Reproducible

A Persuasive Essay: When you have completed your discussion of the overhead, ask students to mark the opinions in the essay with an *O*, and the facts with an *F*. Then urge them to write a short paragraph describing their reaction to the essay. Were they convinced by the writer's argument? Why did they agree or disagree with the essay?

Writing Practice

A Persuasive Essay: To end their introduction to the different types of essays, ask students to write a persuasive essay with at least three paragraphs. Suggested prompts: Persuade your teacher to stop giving your class homework. Convince your teacher to give you an *A*. Persuade your parents to let you make an important decision about your life.

NOTE: After you and your students complete the last lesson in this book, have them revisit their four Writing Practice essays. Based on what they've learned, how would they revise each essay?

Name ______________________________ Date ____________________

A Persuasive Essay

Let Us Have Lettuce!

introduction [According to the United States government, about 31 percent of children from 6 to 19 are overweight. In health class, we learn about the food groups and the importance of eating a variety of foods. Then we go to the cafeteria for a lunch of chicken nuggets and French fries. Throughout the day, we snack on high-sugar and high-fat food from vending machines in school. No wonder so many of us are putting on too much weight! Our school needs to help its students stay healthy by changing the way it offers food to us.]

thesis

body [Kids love to eat pizza and burgers, and our school cafeteria indulges our cravings. But kids also like making their own choices about what they eat. Putting a salad bar in the school cafeteria would give us more healthy meal choices. School cafeterias all across the country have salad bars, and they're a big hit. A high school cafeteria in Palm Beach, Florida, sold over 5,000 salads in two days! School cafeterias in Santa Monica, California, serve organic fresh fruit and vegetables at their salad bars. The city's farmers' market supplies all the produce. Some Santa Monica schools have reported an increase of 1700% in students choosing the salad bars! And Lincoln Elementary School in Olympia, Washington, features an organic salad bar. Although organic food costs more than conventional food, the Lincoln Elementary cafeteria now spends 2 cents less on lunch costs.

Let's face it—vending machines are in schools to stay. A school might keep as much as 40 percent of the money from its machines. This money helps pay for things like special events, uniforms, and textbooks. The schools, and the students, need the money from machines. But why not give us a choice of product there, too? Bring in machines that offer healthier and more nutritious food such as yogurt smoothies and baked potato chips, or even dill pickles!]

conclusion [In addition to teaching us how to solve problems in math, science, and language arts, our school should be teaching us how to make healthy choices in our diets. Having a salad bar in the cafeteria and installing vending machines with healthier snacks would at least give us kids a choice. Maybe not all of us will go for the lettuce and the smoothies, but how can we choose healthy food if it's not even available to us?]

Brainstorming

National Language Arts Standards:

- Uses prewriting strategies to plan written work
- Writes expository compositions
- Identifies and stays on topic

Overhead Transparency

- Brainstorming

Reproducibles

- Topic Web
- Making a List

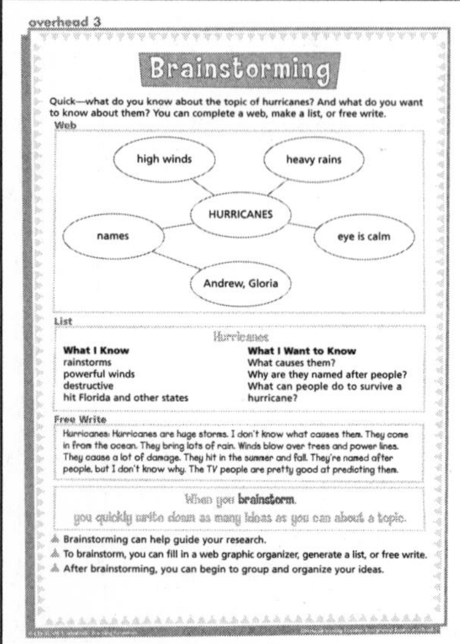

overhead 3

Brainstorming

Quick—what do you know about the topic of hurricanes? And what do you want to know about them? You can complete a web, make a list, or free write.

Web

List

Hurricanes

What I Know	What I Want to Know
rainstorms	What causes them?
powerful winds	Why are they named after people?
destructive	What can people do to survive a hurricane?
hit Florida and other states	

Free Write

Hurricanes: Hurricanes are huge storms. I don't know what causes them. They come in from the ocean. They bring lots of rain. Winds blow over trees and power lines. They cause a lot of damage. They hit in the summer and fall. They're named after people, but I don't know why. The TV people are pretty good at predicting them.

When you **brainstorm**, you quickly write down as many ideas as you can about a topic.

- Brainstorming can help guide your research.
- To brainstorm, you can fill in a web graphic organizer, generate a list, or free write.
- After brainstorming, you can begin to group and organize your ideas.

Purpose

To explore different methods of brainstorming ideas for essays

Brainstorming is an important part of the process of writing an essay because it helps students see what they know about a topic and what they need to find out. By completing webs, making lists, or writing freely, students can let their natural curiosity lead them into interesting avenues of exploration about a topic.

With this lesson, students begin the process of writing two different essays. The first one is an essay about dogs that you'll guide them through as a whole-class activity using the reproducibles. The other essay is about a topic of your (or students') choice, which they'll work on independently.

Launching Activity: Brainstorming (Overhead 3)

This activity introduces three different methods of brainstorming for students to try: using a web, making a list, and free writing. The method a student chooses may depend upon his or her learning style as well as on the type of essay being written. They may even develop their own methods of recording ideas while they brainstorm, and that's okay, too.

The questions for students to consider about a topic as they brainstorm are: What do I know about this topic? and What do I want to know about this topic?

Above all, no matter which method they use, students should not censor themselves as they brainstorm. Later, they can consider their ideas, group them, and discard any that don't seem to fit. In the case of expository and persuasive essays, this final group of ideas serves as a place for students to begin their research.

Before displaying the overhead, ask students to quickly write down everything they know about hurricanes, and what they would like to know. Allow about ten minutes for this activity. After students finish, explain that they were doing a method of brainstorming called free writing. Then present the brainstorming information and examples on the overhead. Have students share any of their ideas or questions that don't appear in the examples.

Show them how to include their ideas or questions in the web, the list, and in free writing examples on the overhead. Emphasize that they shouldn't worry about writing complete sentences, capitalization, or punctuation. The important thing is to write down enough information so later they'll be able to remember what they were thinking.

Student Reproducibles

Make extra copies of both reproducibles for students to keep in their notebooks. Also store extra copies in your Writing Center. With these reproducibles, students embark on the process of planning, organizing, and writing an expository essay about working dogs. The Answer Key on page 49 provides sample answers for each step of the process, as well as a sample essay.

Topic Web: As students brainstorm to complete the web, circulate among them in case anyone gets stuck. Have a couple of ideas from the Answer Key ready to toss out.

Making a List: Go over the lists with students. Help them separate any ideas or questions that might appear under the wrong heading.

NOTE: Students may also brainstorm by using free writing, which they can do on sheets of paper. However, encourage them to practice all the methods before settling on one.

Writing Practice

Now students begin the process of writing an expository essay independently. You may want to select one topic for everyone to work on, present several topics for students to choose from, or work with the class in selecting one topic. Then, armed with the topic, have students brainstorm ideas and questions about it.

Name ______________________________ Date ____________________

Topic Web

To brainstorm ideas, complete the web. Remember: You can add more ovals to the web. Connect each oval to the center oval or to another outside oval.

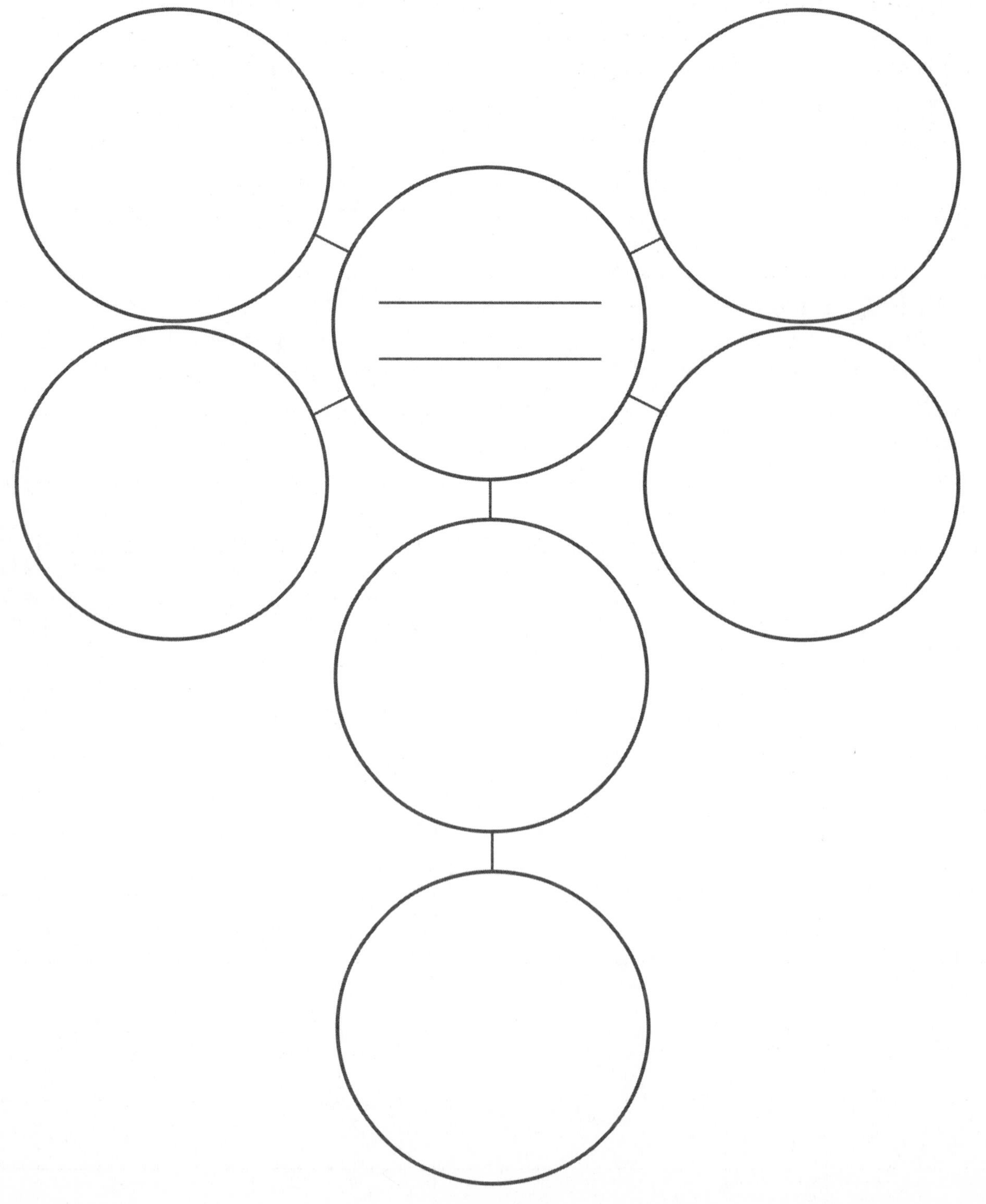

Name ______________________ Date ______________________

Making a List

You can write a list to brainstorm. Write down what you know and what you want to find out.

What I Know	What I Want to Know

The Thesis

Purpose

To explain the importance of a thesis and how to write a strong thesis

The thesis of an essay should ring with significance. If students can't produce a good thesis, they will have difficulty developing their essay. They'll find themselves rambling about the topic because their thesis offers them no direction. Another problem is that students sometimes present basic facts as a thesis. They fail to realize that facts are not debatable in the same way that an arguable point is. It's important for students to understand that creating a good thesis is a process and that they may need to rework it several times.

National Language Arts Standards:

- Uses prewriting strategies to plan written work
- Uses strategies to draft and revise written work
- Writes expository compositions
- Identifies and stays on topic

Launching Activity: The Thesis (Overhead 4)

Begin by reminding students about the brainstorming they did on hurricanes in the previous lesson. Review the Brainstorming overhead to refresh their memories about the methods and ideas generated. Point out the ways in which ideas and/or questions about hurricanes' names appear in the web, the list, and the free writing. Explain that the next step in writing an essay is creating a thesis. Tell students that they'll be learning how to use the information about hurricanes' names to create a thesis.

Since the information in the web and the free writing doesn't appear as questions, it's important to show students how to generate a question from the material. Here's what you might say: *I've decided I want you all to write about hurricanes' names. That's still a big topic. To narrow it down, I think about a question I have about hurricanes' names. For instance, Why are names given to hurricanes? Answering this question will help you develop a thesis for your essay.*

Display the overhead, and read the introduction. Guide students through the development of the thesis from an essay question. Make sure they can see the differences between each of the statements and the progressive development to the final thesis statement.

Then go over the definition and information on the overhead. After posing the essay question to students, give them a few minutes to think about it. You may want to start the process by modeling your own thinking: *First, I wrote this down: We should recycle aluminum cans and glass bottles because [blank]. Then, I thought, we should recycle because it's good. But why is recycling good?*

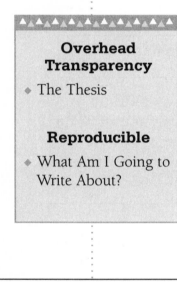

Overhead Transparency

- The Thesis

Reproducible

- What Am I Going to Write About?

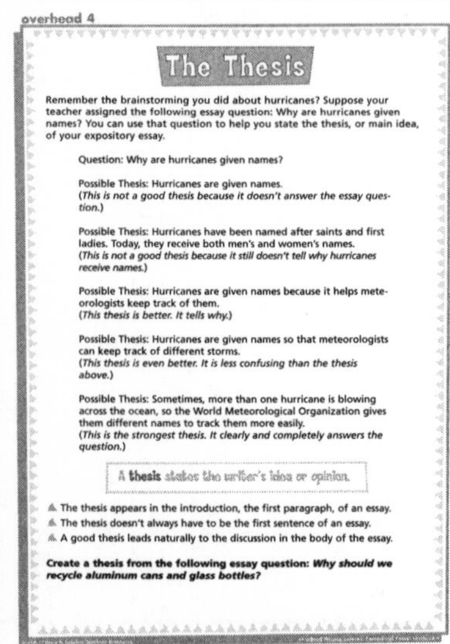

overhead 4

The Thesis

Remember the brainstorming you did about hurricanes? Suppose your teacher assigned the following essay question: Why are hurricanes given names? You can use that question to help you state the thesis, or main idea, of your expository essay.

Question: Why are hurricanes given names?

Possible Thesis: Hurricanes are given names.
(*This is not a good thesis because it doesn't answer the essay question.*)

Possible Thesis: Hurricanes have been named after saints and first ladies. Today, they receive both men's and women's names.
(*This is not a good thesis because it still doesn't tell why hurricanes receive names.*)

Possible Thesis: Hurricanes are given names because it helps meteorologists keep track of them.
(*This thesis is better. It tells why.*)

Possible Thesis: Hurricanes are given names so that meteorologists can keep track of different storms.
(*This thesis is even better. It is less confusing than the thesis above.*)

Possible Thesis: Sometimes, more than one hurricane is blowing across the ocean, so the World Meteorological Organization gives them different names to track them more easily.
(*This is the strongest thesis. It clearly and completely answers the question.*)

A **thesis** states the writer's idea or opinion.

- The thesis appears in the introduction, the first paragraph, of an essay.
- The thesis doesn't always have to be the first sentence of an essay.
- A good thesis leads naturally to the discussion in the body of the essay.

Create a thesis from the following essay question: *Why should we recycle aluminum cans and glass bottles?*

Write on the board students' responses about the benefits of recycling. Use the responses to complete the thesis you modeled, for example: *We should recycle aluminum cans and glass bottles because that creates less garbage.* Continue to ask for students' input about how to make the thesis stronger until the class reaches a consensus.

Student Reproducible

What Am I Going to Write About?: This reproducible builds upon the reproducibles (pages 18 and 19) on dogs that students completed in the previous lesson. They continue the process of planning their essays with this reproducible. If students are overwhelmed by the amount of material they generated in their brainstorming sessions, this reproducible will help them focus their thoughts and ideas.

Writing Practice

Now it's time for students to write a thesis for the expository essay topic or topics you introduced in the previous lesson on brainstorming. Move among students as they work in case anyone is struggling to transform their ideas and questions into a strong thesis. Also, meet with students individually to discuss their thesis statements. Ask them to tell you how they used their brainstorming ideas to create the thesis. Help students fine-tune as necessary.

Enriching the Lesson

Have students pull out their examples of each type of essay (reproducible pages 9, 11, 13, 15). Ask them to look at the thesis in each essay and note its position in the introductory paragraph and its length. Challenge them to restate each thesis as a possible essay question.

Name ______________________________ Date ____________________

What Am I Going to Write About?

In the last lesson, you brainstormed about the topic of dogs. If you were going to write an expository essay about dogs, how would you begin?

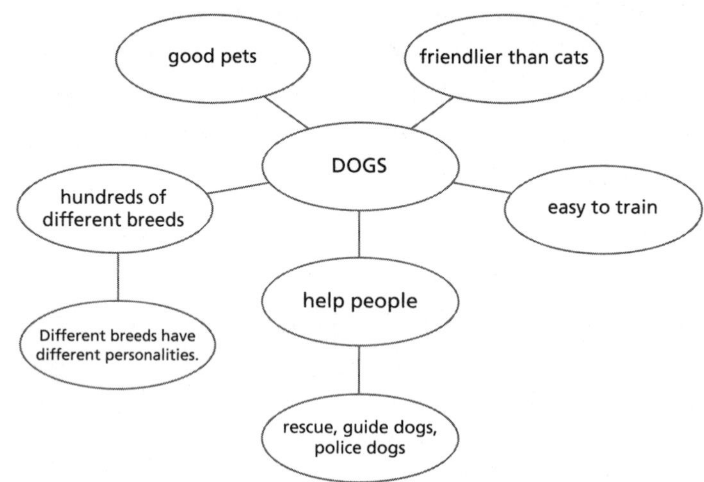

1. Look over the information you brainstormed.
Which idea really interests you?
Does a big idea jump out at you?
Which ideas have you already developed by adding another oval to the web?

2. Choose one of the ideas from the web.
Dogs help people.

3. Change the statement into a question.

____

4. Use the question to write a thesis. You can write on another sheet of paper in case you want to keep revising your thesis.

____

____

____

____

5. Does any of the information in the web help support your thesis?

____

Outlining

Purpose

To introduce the concept of outlining to organize the ideas in an essay

Now that students have a thesis in place, they can move on to create an outline to help them organize their ideas and to guide their research. An outline can spotlight any blank areas in their arguments. Although an outline is an orderly plan, students are sometimes confused about the sequence of Roman numerals and capital letters. The reproducible Organizing Your Ideas (page 25) provides a template for them to use.

National Language Arts Standards:

- Uses prewriting strategies to plan written work
- Uses strategies to draft and revise written work
- Writes expository compositions
- Identifies and stays on topic

Launching Activity: Outlining (Overhead 5)

This overhead continues the exploration of writing an expository essay on naming hurricanes. In the previous lesson, students saw the thesis evolve from a question into several possible thesis statements. In this lesson, they learn how to place that thesis within a framework. You may want to briefly review those thesis statements.

Display the overhead, and read through the introduction and sample outline with students. Make sure they understand the connection to the previous lesson. As you read the bulleted information, point out the corresponding material on the sample outline (Roman numerals and so on). Emphasize that this is a basic outline, which can be lengthened. Any outlines they create will always show the number and order of paragraphs in their essay. The conclusion is undeveloped because they haven't yet begun writing. It will follow once students develop their ideas.

Then discuss the questions at the bottom of the overhead. Encourage students to think critically about question 1 by asking: *Is there anything you want to know about hurricanes' names that might not fit into these two main points? Is the writer forgetting any main points?*

If students disagree about where the supporting details should go in the outline, draw them out to assess their thinking. Several of the choices could be placed under either section II or section III. Answers for question 2: Until 1979…(II.); The 2007 list…(III.); The names of really destructive…(II. or III.); The names of …(II. or III.).

Student Reproducible

Make extra copies for students to keep in their notebooks and store some in your Writing Center.

Overhead Transparency

- Outlining

Reproducible

- Organizing Your Ideas

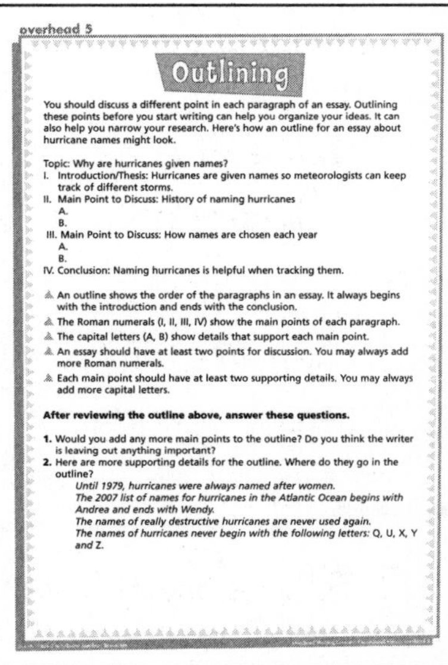

overhead 5

Outlining

You should discuss a different point in each paragraph of an essay. Outlining these points before you start writing can help you organize your ideas. It can also help you narrow your research. Here's how an outline for an essay about hurricane names might look.

Topic: Why are hurricanes given names?

I. Introduction/Thesis: Hurricanes are given names so meteorologists can keep track of different storms.

II. Main Point to Discuss: History of naming hurricanes
  A.
  B.

III. Main Point to Discuss: How names are chosen each year
  A.
  B.

IV. Conclusion: Naming hurricanes is helpful when tracking them.

- An outline shows the order of the paragraphs in an essay. It always begins with the introduction and ends with the conclusion.
- The Roman numerals (I, II, III, IV) show the main points of each paragraph.
- The capital letters (A, B) show details that support each main point.
- An essay should have at least two points for discussion. You may always add more Roman numerals.
- Each main point should have at least two supporting details. You may always add more capital letters.

After reviewing the outline above, answer these questions.

1. Would you add any more main points to the outline? Do you think the writer is leaving out anything important?
2. Here are more supporting details for the outline. Where do they go in the outline?
   Until 1979, hurricanes were always named after women.
   The 2007 list of names for hurricanes in the Atlantic Ocean begins with Andrea and ends with Wendy.
   The names of really destructive hurricanes are never used again.
   The names of hurricanes never begin with the following letters: Q, U, X, Y and Z.

Organizing Your Ideas: This activity extends students' work on the thesis statements about dogs they produced in the previous lesson. At this point, they shouldn't be concerned with what they know, or don't know, about these types of working dogs. Emphasize that the important thing is for them to set a plan in place. Then they will know where and how to look for details about each group of dogs. On the other hand, if students can use their own knowledge to flesh out details in the outline, that's terrific.

Writing Practice

Now it's time for students to apply what they've learned about outlining to their own expository essays on the topic(s) you've assigned. Again, set aside time for individual conferences to make sure students are on the right track. Also, use class time to discuss any questions students have or any problems you've noticed in the conferences.

Name ______________________________ Date ____________________

Organizing Your Ideas

Topic: ____________________

I. Introduction/Thesis: ______________________________

____

II. Main Point to Discuss: ______________________________

____

A. ______________________________

____

B. ______________________________

____

III. Main Point to Discuss: ______________________________

____

A. ______________________________

____

B. ______________________________

____

IV. Main Point to Discuss: ______________________________

____

A. ______________________________

____

B. ______________________________

____

V. Conclusion: ______________________________

____

Note-Taking and Quotations

National Language Arts Standards:

- Uses prewriting strategies to plan written work, including taking notes
- Uses several sources of information
- Uses strategies to draft and revise written work
- Writes expository compositions
- Identifies and stays on topic

Overhead Transparency

- Note-Taking and Quotations

Reproducibles

- Note-Taking Tips
- A Quote Sandwich
- Setting Off Quotations in an Essay

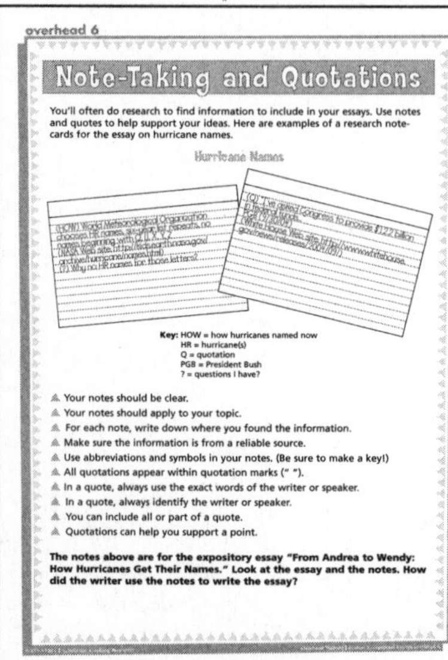
overhead 6

Note-Taking and Quotations

You'll often do research to find information to include in your essays. Use notes and quotes to help support your ideas. Here are examples of a research note-cards for the essay on hurricane names.

Hurricane Names

Key: HOW = how hurricanes named now
HR = hurricane(s)
Q = quotation
PGB = President Bush
? = questions I have?

- Your notes should be clear.
- Your notes should apply to your topic.
- For each note, write down where you found the information.
- Make sure the information is from a reliable source.
- Use abbreviations and symbols in your notes. (Be sure to make a key!)
- All quotations appear within quotation marks (" ").
- In a quote, always use the exact words of the writer or speaker.
- In a quote, always identify the writer or speaker.
- You can include all or part of a quote.
- Quotations can help you support a point.

The notes above are for the expository essay "From Andrea to Wendy: How Hurricanes Get Their Names." Look at the essay and the notes. How did the writer use the notes to write the essay?

◆ Purpose ◆

To understand how to take effective notes and to quote accurately

Note-taking seems to come naturally to a few orderly souls, but most students need to have the principles explained to them. Some students may feel that there's no sense in doing research and taking notes because they're unable to decipher them later.

Part of their note-taking will include quotations. Many students struggle with how to use them properly and they experience several common problems. They often include a quotation without introducing it, so the quotation seems to come out of nowhere. Also, some students fail to discuss interesting quotes fully and they sometimes place a quotation at the end of a paragraph. Besides potentially affecting the transition to the next paragraph, this placement often means that the quotation isn't explained well enough. Students' essays may contain too many quotations, or not enough of them. And finally, perhaps most serious of all, students fail to use quotation marks and thus commit plagiarism. They need to understand—sooner rather than later—exactly what plagiarism is and why it's unacceptable.

NOTE: It's best to cover this lesson in at least two days. Focus on taking notes on the first day, and move on to quotations on the second day. Students will increasingly be using these essential skills. Right now, we're building the foundation for writing research papers that include footnotes and bibliographies.

The Note-Taking and Quotations overhead shows examples of notes for the expository essay "From Andrea to Wendy: How Hurricanes Get Their Names." Students will also need a copy of the essay (page 9) for both days of this activity.

Day One—Taking Notes (Overhead 6)

Launching Activity: Go over the information on the overhead about taking notes. Then discuss the sample notes. You may want to explain that the source of the second note is FEMA, the Federal Emergency Management Agency. This government agency is responsible for going into communities and managing emergencies such as hurricanes. Pose questions such as the following: *Are all of the notes about how hurricanes are named? What do you think about the sources the writer found? Do they seem reliable to you? What does the question mark mean? Do you think some notes contain more important information than others do? How could you show this in the notes? How do you think looking at your brainstorming ideas and your outlines could help you write better notes?*

Point out that notes are informal. Students may have chosen different abbreviations and symbols to use; the most important thing is that the person taking the notes understands them. Then have students turn to their copies of the actual essay. Seeing how the information in the notes appears in the actual essay will help them understand the note-taking process. Discuss the question at the bottom of the overhead. Answer: The first note appears in the second paragraph (the body). The second note appears in the third paragraph (the body). Information from the quotation appears in the final paragraph (the conclusion).

Student Reproducibles

Make extra copies of this reproducible for students and also store some in your Writing Center.

Note-Taking Tips: Feel free to add your own tips to the reproducible since students need to learn to work within the guidelines of different teachers.

You may want to display the overhead as you go over the points on this reproducible; the sample notecard can help reinforce the note-taking tips.

Day Two—Quotations (Overhead 6)

Launching Activity: Quotations can add a spark to essays. They can introduce startling information or be used to support generalizations that a writer makes. But no matter how quotations are used, they must be recorded word for word and cited accurately.

After sharing the information about quotations on the overhead, write on the board the full text of the quote by President Bush: "I've asked Congress to provide $12.2 billion in federal funds to respond to these storms." Ask the class to decide how to incorporate the full quote into the conclusion of the essay (page 9). Write their decision on the board, showing them the correct style and punctuation for including the quotation.

Student Reproducibles

Duplicate copies of these reproducibles for students to keep in their notebooks for reference. Also make extra copies to store in your Writing Center.

A Quote Sandwich: Students may be tempted to incorporate several long quotations to pad their essays. Emphasize that quotations should be used to help develop the essay, and not to take up space.

Setting Off Quotations in an Essay: Even when students copy a quotation word for word, they may have difficulty knowing how to punctuate and place it in the text of their essay. This reproducible shows three examples—complete quotations that are both long and short, and a part of a quotation. Discuss the examples with students.

Now it's time for students to research and take notes for their "working dogs" essays. Have them carry all three reproducibles (pages 29–31) with them to the school library (or the Writing Center if you've stocked it with research material about working dogs) as they make notes and look for quotations.

▲ Writing Practice

Tell students to research the topic they've been working on in the Writing Practice essays. Set up an appointment for your class with the school or public librarian, or have students work independently on this as homework. Review students' notes with them to make sure they're using them effectively.

▲ Teaching Tip

If you suspect you have a plagiarized paper, type a ringing phrase from it into a search engine such as Google™. Finding the source of the paper can be startlingly easy, since free papers are the most popular and the simplest to locate online. Unfortunately, it's possible for a student to locate, copy, adapt, and print out an essay in under fifteen minutes.

As soon as you spot possible plagiarism, set up a conference with the student. He or she may be unaware of the plagiarism. For instance, the student may have inadvertently omitted quotation marks. This may be the result of poor note-taking, or it may indicate a misunderstanding of how to use quotations. Work with the student to build up proficiency in these skills. In the case of intentional plagiarism, try to find out the cause. It may be external, such as family problems. It may be internal: A student may feel overwhelmed by the process. If that's the case, pinpoint the areas in the process where he or she is faltering. Always encourage students to come to you for help whenever they feel stuck or confused.

As teachers, we have to be as technologically savvy as our students are. Things have changed since many of us typed our high school and college essays.

Name ______________________________ Date ______________

Note-Taking Tips

1. Take notes with your topic in mind. Stay focused by looking at your brainstorming material and outline often.

2. Abbreviate to save time. Use the first letter(s) of a name: GW for George Washington. Make a key so you'll remember what the abbreviations mean.

3. Mark important notes with a symbol, such as a checkmark (✓) or an asterisk (*).

4. Include a space between different notes. Don't run your notes together in paragraph form. You should be able to glance quickly at your notes to find the information you need.

5. Copy down quotations correctly. Always write down the name of the book or article, the author, and the page number(s) or Web site(s).

6. Avoid copying long quotations now. Write down enough so you'll be able to find the quote when it's time to write your essay.

7. Jot down any question you have.

8. Make a note of any patterns you see. They could be important. For example, you may notice that an author mentions the same story or fable several times in an article. Write down the title.

9. Use your own wording in notes. But use more formal wording in your essay.

10. Read over your notes occasionally. Think about what you notice. How does the information in your notes connect?

Name ______________________ Date ______________

A Quote Sandwich

A quotation in an essay looks a little like a sandwich. Your own writing "sandwiches" the quotation like two pieces of bread.

<u>The Witch of Blackbird Pond</u> tells about the challenges Kit faces when she must move to a new home in a new place. The move from the lush, green tropics to the cold shoreline of Connecticut didn't excite Kit. Seeing Connecticut for the first time was disappointing. The author Elizabeth George Speare describes Kit's feelings:

"The bleak line of shore surrounding the gray harbour was a disheartening contrast to the shimmering green and white that fringed the turquoise bay of Barbados, which was her home."

Words such as <u>bleak</u> and <u>disheartening</u> make Kit's feelings for her new home clear. Cold Connecticut can't compare to the warm beauty of Barbados. Obviously, Kit will have a hard time adjusting to her new home.

Name ______________________________ Date ______________

Setting Off Quotations in an Essay

Here is how a long, full quotation would look in an essay.

The Witch of Blackbird Pond tells about the challenges Kit faces when she must move to a new home in a new place. The move from the lush, green tropics to the cold shoreline of Connecticut didn't excite her. Seeing Connecticut for the first time was disappointing. The author Elizabeth George Speare describes Kit's feelings:

> The bleak line of shore surrounding the gray harbour was a disheartening contrast to the shimmering green and white that fringed the turquoise bay of Barbados which was her home.

Words such as *bleak* and *disheartening* make Kit's feelings for her new home clear. Cold Connecticut can't compare to the warm beauty of Barbados. Obviously, Kit will have a hard time adjusting to her new home.

▲ If the quotation is longer than three lines, use this style.

- A colon (:) introduces the quotation.
- Set off the quotation from the rest of the paragraph.
- Indent the quotation 10 spaces on the right and left margins.
- Don't use quotation marks.

Here is how a full, but short, quotation would look. It's less than three lines.

The Witch of Blackbird Pond tells about the challenges Kit faces when she must move to a new home. The move from the lush, green tropics to the cold shoreline of Connecticut didn't excite her. Author Elizabeth George Speare describes Kit's feelings: "She didn't want to admit how disappointing she found this first glimpse of America." The word *disappointing* makes Kit's feelings for her new home clear. Obviously, she will have a hard time adjusting to Connecticut.

▲ If the quotation is less than three lines, use this style.

- A colon (:) introduces the quotation.
- Place quotation marks around the quotation.

You can also use part of a quotation in an essay.

Kit felt that the Connecticut shoreline was a "disheartening contrast" to the beauty of her home in Barbados.

▲ If you use part of a quotation, use this style.

- Set off the part of the quotation with quotation marks.

Introduction

National Language Arts Standards:

- Uses prewriting strategies to plan written work
- Uses strategies to draft and revise written work
- Writes expository compositions
- Identifies and stays on topic

Overhead Transparency

- Introduction

Reproducible

- Ladies and Gentlemen, A Preview of Coming Attractions!

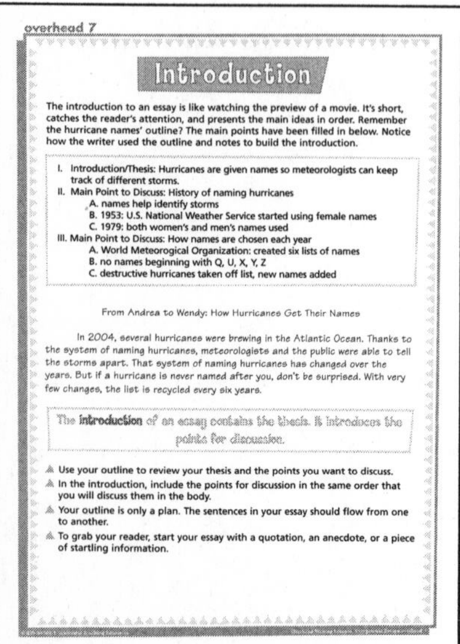

overhead 7

Introduction

The introduction to an essay is like watching the preview of a movie. It's short, catches the reader's attention, and presents the main ideas in order. Remember the hurricane names' outline? The main points have been filled in below. Notice how the writer used the outline and notes to build the introduction.

I. Introduction/Thesis: Hurricanes are given names so meteorologists can keep track of different storms.
II. Main Point to Discuss: History of naming hurricanes
  A. names help identify storms
  B. 1953: U.S. National Weather Service started using female names
  C. 1979: both women's and men's names used
III. Main Point to Discuss: How names are chosen each year
  A. World Meteorogical Organization: created six lists of names
  B. no names beginning with Q, U, X, Y, Z
  C. destructive hurricanes taken off list, new names added

From Andrea to Wendy: How Hurricanes Get Their Names

In 2004, several hurricanes were brewing in the Atlantic Ocean. Thanks to the system of naming hurricanes, meteorologists and the public were able to tell the storms apart. That system of naming hurricanes has changed over the years. But if a hurricane is never named after you, don't be surprised. With very few changes, the list is recycled every six years.

The **introduction** of an essay contains the thesis. It introduces the points for discussion.

- Use your outline to review your thesis and the points you want to discuss.
- In the introduction, include the points for discussion in the same order that you will discuss them in the body.
- Your outline is only a plan. The sentences in your essay should flow from one to another.
- To grab your reader, start your essay with a quotation, an anecdote, or a piece of startling information.

◆ Purpose ◆

To learn about the form and function of the opening paragraph of an essay

As students learn about writing a solid introduction to an essay, they'll make good use of their outlines. The introduction reflects the writer's grasp of where his or her essay is going. An unclear introduction usually indicates that the writer hasn't gone through all the necessary steps before writing: brainstorming, outlining, and taking notes.

This lesson gives students plenty of practice in translating information from an outline and their notes to an introduction. In the overhead activity, they see the transformation of the hurricane names' outline from the previous lesson into an introduction. The reproducible guides them through the creation of an introduction from their outlines on dogs, also building from the previous lesson, and students also continue to work on their own expository essays.

Launching Activity: Introduction (Overhead 7)

Discuss the definition and information about the introduction with students. Then review the outline at the top of the overhead. Question them about their thoughts on the introduction. Did they find it engaging? Would it make them want to read the rest of the essay? Do they think it meets the requirements of a good introduction? If it doesn't, then what is missing? How does the wording of the introduction differ from the outline?

Then read this alternate introduction to students: *Meteorologists use different names to keep track of hurricanes. The names have an interesting history. Some hurricane names are never used again.*

Ask students what they think of it. How does it compare to the first introduction? (The thesis is the first sentence; the second sentence covers one of the main points for discussion, but the third sentence is a detail rather than a main point.) However, what students should really notice is the dryness of the prose. Emphasize that an outline is the bare bones of an essay. The ideas and details must be developed so that the relationship between the sentences creates a flow.

Student Reproducible

Ladies and Gentlemen, A Preview of Coming Attractions! Before students begin work, go over the checklist at the bottom of the reproducible.

Explain that they will probably go through several drafts before they feel they're satisfied with their introductions. After reviewing students' work, share their results. It will be illuminating for students to see how differently the same information can be expressed.

Writing Practice

Have students break out the outlines and notes for their expository essays and use them to write an introduction. While they work, keep the overhead for this lesson on display so they can refer to it. You may want to have pairs of students exchange introductions so they can give and receive feedback. Encourage them to be constructive critics. They can use the checklist at the bottom of the reproducible on page 34 as a guide. Ask a pair to share their responses with the rest of the class. Sit in with them to model more productive responses as necessary.

Name ______________________________ Date ______________

Ladies and Gentlemen, A Preview of Coming Attractions!

Pull out the outline you completed for working dogs. Use it to write an introduction to an essay. Work on another sheet of paper. When you're satisfied with your introduction, copy it on the lines below.

Remember—an introduction offers an exciting preview of your essay!

Checklist for a strong introduction:

- Does it contain the thesis?
- Are the main points presented in order?
- Is it clear and engaging?
- Have I checked spelling and grammar?

Body of the Essay

◆ Purpose ◆

To understand how to develop the body of an essay

Even though students complete outlines, they may veer off the topic in the heat of writing. Creating a topic sentence for each paragraph in the body as well as sentences that supply supporting details can help students stay on track. This will also enable students to see if the topic sentence of each paragraph connects to the thesis of the essay.

National Language Arts Standards:

- ▲ Uses prewriting strategies to plan written work
- ▲ Uses strategies to draft and revise written work
- ▲ Writes expository compositions
- ▲ Identifies and stays on topic

▲ Launching Activity: Body of the Essay (Overhead 8)

Tell students they'll be learning about how to write the longest portion of the essay, the body. That's where they'll discuss the main points in their essay. Before displaying the overhead, review the Outlining overhead. Then present the Body of the Essay overhead. Read the material on the overhead, but stop before the questions at the bottom. Discuss in a general way how they think the essay is developing and progressing. Then ask students to read the essay again before moving on to the questions. Answers: 1. second and third paragraphs 2. second paragraph: People have been naming hurricanes for hundreds of years. third paragraph: The World Meteorological Organization has created a list of names for hurricanes in the Atlantic Ocean. 3.

Sample answers: second paragraph: Then Australian meteorologist, Clement Wragge, began giving women's names to hurricanes in the late 1800s. third paragraph: The lists are alphabetical, but they don't include the letters *Q*, *U*, *X*, *Y*, or *Z*. 4. Possible answer: The second paragraph tells about the history of hurricane naming and how it's changed. The third paragraph tells about how hurricanes are named today.

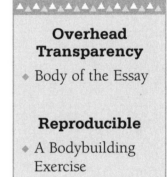

Overhead Transparency

◆ Body of the Essay

Reproducible

◆ A Bodybuilding Exercise

▲ Student Reproducible

Duplicate extra copies of this reproducible for students to keep in their notebooks and to store in your Writing Center.

A Bodybuilding Exercise: You may find that you need to review the structure of a paragraph with students. Although the paragraphs in the body support the thesis of the essay, each paragraph must contain its own main idea and details. This reproducible will help students in crafting solid paragraphs with complete and related sentences.

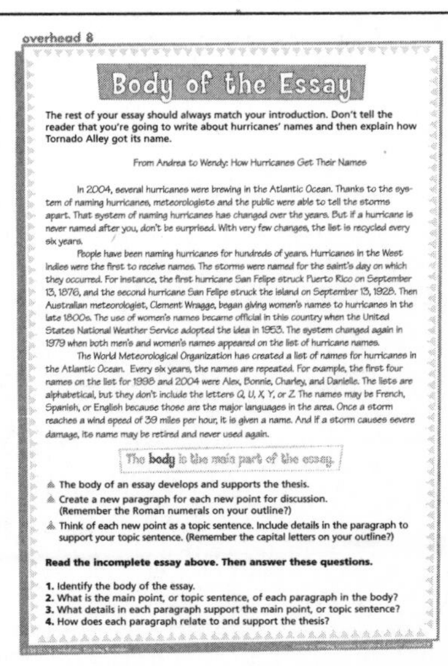

overhead 8

Body of the Essay

The rest of your essay should always match your introduction. Don't tell the reader that you're going to write about hurricanes' names and then explain how Tornado Alley got its name.

From Andrea to Wendy: How Hurricanes Get Their Names

In 2004, several hurricanes were brewing in the Atlantic Ocean. Thanks to the system of naming hurricanes, meteorologists and the public were able to tell the storms apart. That system of naming hurricanes has changed over the years. But if a hurricane is never named after you, don't be surprised. With very few changes, the list is recycled every six years.

People have been naming hurricanes for hundreds of years. Hurricanes in the West Indies were the first to receive names. The storms were named for the saint's day on which they occurred. For instance, the first hurricane San Felipe struck Puerto Rico on September 13, 1876, and the second hurricane San Felipe struck the island on September 13, 1928. Then Australian meteorologist, Clement Wragge, began giving women's names to hurricanes in the late 1800s. The use of women's names became official in this country when the United States National Weather Service adopted the idea in 1953. The system changed again in 1979 when both men's and women's names appeared on the list of hurricane names.

The World Meteorological Organization has created a list of names for hurricanes in the Atlantic Ocean. Every six years, the names are repeated. For example, the first four names on the list for 1998 and 2004 were Alex, Bonnie, Charley, and Danielle. The lists are alphabetical, but they don't include the letters Q, U, X, Y, or Z. The names may be French, Spanish, or English because those are the major languages in the area. Once a storm reaches a wind speed of 39 miles per hour, it is given a name. And if a storm causes severe damage, its name may be retired and never used again.

The **body** is the main part of the essay.

- **The body of an essay develops and supports the thesis.**
- **Create a new paragraph for each new point for discussion. (Remember the Roman numerals on your outline?)**
- **Think of each new point as a topic sentence. Include details in the paragraph to support your topic sentence. (Remember the capital letters on your outline?)**

Read the incomplete essay above. Then answer these questions.

1. Identify the body of the essay.
2. What is the main point, or topic sentence, of each paragraph in the body?
3. What details in each paragraph support the main point, or topic sentence?
4. How does each paragraph relate to and support the thesis?

For practice, have them complete the chart using their outline and notes for their working dogs essay from previous lessons. You may want to model your thinking about writing the first paragraph. Tell students: *In the body of my essay, the first paragraph will be about rescue dogs. I want to talk about which breeds make good rescue dogs, and I want to discuss the types of jobs rescue dogs do. I also want to make sure that my topic sentence and details connect back to my thesis in the introduction. Here's what I was thinking about for the topic sentence: Rescue dogs work long hours in difficult conditions, so they must remain calm and focused. Then I can use details about the best breeds for rescue work and their characteristics, and more information about the work they actually do.*

Then have students use the reproducible to write the body for their own working dogs essays.

Writing Practice

Have students continue to work on their expository essays. In this step of the process, ask them to complete the A Bodybuilding Exercise reproducible on the next page for the body of the essay. You may want to display some of the reproducibles that were created above for the working dogs essay.

Name ____________________ Date ____________________

A Bodybuilding Exercise

You can use this chart to help you write the body of your essay. Each paragraph in the body should have its own topic sentence and details that support it.

Paragraph 1 of Body:

Main Idea:

Detail:

Detail:

Detail:

Paragraph 2 of Body:

Main Idea:

Detail:

Detail:

Detail:

Paragraph 3 of Body:

Main Idea:

Detail:

Detail:

Detail:

Conclusion

Purpose

To understand the importance of a strong conclusion

Conclusions in early essays can be deadly, since students are learning so many new skills. Just getting to the end of an essay can be a fairly heroic act on their part. This skill will come in time. And although it may take students a while to write a really strong conclusion, it's essential that they know a conclusion is more than repeating the thesis word for word. It will be tempting for young writers to speed through the conclusion to complete their essay. But to wind up the essay successfully, they'll need to use everything they put into their essay, and then some—a quote or a fact—to make a vivid impression on the reader. The conclusion will be their final word on the topic.

National Language Arts Standards:

- Uses prewriting strategies to plan written work
- Uses strategies to draft and revise written work
- Writes expository compositions
- Identifies and stays on topic

Launching Activity: Conclusion (Overhead 9)

This activity concludes the essay about hurricanes' names that you and your students have seen in its various stages of development. The conclusion, the final paragraph, incorporates and synthesizes the thesis and main points.

Introduce the information on the overhead, and then read aloud the essay on hurricane names. Point out that the concluding paragraph echoes the introduction in the discussion of the 2004 hurricane season. Then discuss the questions at the bottom of the overhead. Answers will vary, depending upon students' responses.

Also revisit the Outlining overhead so that students can see how the conclusion has changed. Remind them that this is because the outline was written before the topic was researched and developed. It's important for them to remember that their outline is only a plan, and that plans change. What they write in their introduction and body will drive the development of the conclusion.

Overhead Transparency

- Conclusion

Reproducible

- The Final Zing!

Student Reproducible

The Final Zing!: Students will continue to work on their working dogs essays with this reproducible. Remind them to consult the reproducibles they've already completed in previous lessons. If their notes don't contain an interesting or surprising fact or a quote, allow time for them to examine the research material you've placed in the Writing Center. Then students can complete their essay with a conclusion.

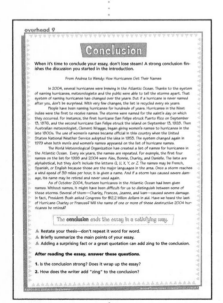

overhead 9

Conclusion

When it's time to conclude your essay, don't lose steam! A strong conclusion finishes the discussion you started in the introduction.

From Andrea to Wendy: How Hurricanes Get Their Names

In 2004, several hurricanes were brewing in the Atlantic Ocean. Thanks to the system of naming hurricanes, meteorologists and the public were able to tell the storms apart. That system of naming hurricanes has changed over the years. But if a hurricane is never named after you, don't be surprised. With very few changes, the list is recycled every six years.

People have been naming hurricanes for hundreds of years. Hurricanes in the West Indies were the first to receive names. The storms were named for the saint's day on which they occurred. For instance, the first hurricane San Felipe struck Puerto Rico on September 13, 1876, and the second hurricane San Felipe struck the island on September 13, 1928. Then Australian meteorologist, Clement Wragge, began giving women's names to hurricanes in the late 1800s. The use of women's names became official in this country when the United States National Weather Service adopted the idea in 1953. The system changed again in 1979 when both men's and women's names appeared on the list of hurricane names.

The World Meteorological Organization has created a list of names for hurricanes in the Atlantic Ocean. Every six years, the names are repeated. For example, the first four names on the list for 1998 and 2004 were Alex, Bonnie, Charley, and Danielle. The lists are alphabetical, but they don't include the letters Q, U, X, Y, or Z. The names may be French, Spanish, or English because those are the major languages in the area. Once a storm reaches a wind speed of 39 miles per hour, it is given a name. And if a storm has caused severe damage, its name may be retired and never used again.

As of October 2004, fourteen hurricanes in the Atlantic Ocean had been given names. Without names, it might have been difficult for us to distinguish between some of these storms. Several of them—Charley, Frances, Jeanne, and Ivan—caused severe damage. In fact, President Bush asked Congress for $12.2 billion dollars in aid. Have we heard the last of Hurricane Charley or Frances? Will the name of one or more of these destructive 2004 hurricanes be retired?

The **conclusion** ends the essay in a satisfying way.

- Restate your thesis—don't repeat it word for word.
- Briefly summarize the main points of your essay.
- Adding a surprising fact or a great quotation can add zing to the conclusion.

After reading the essay, answer these questions.

1. Is the conclusion strong? Does it wrap up the essay?

2. How does the writer add "zing" to the conclusion?

Writing Practice

Now students have the chance to pull everything together and complete a draft of their expository essays. Remind them they will have time to revise and edit their work in later lessons.

NOTE: Some people suggest that writers complete the body of an essay first and then write the introduction and conclusion since the meat of the argument is found in the body. At this stage, it's more helpful to guide students through the process step by step, from brainstorming to editing. We've tried to encourage students to rethink their work at every stage of the process and to suggest that changes are a natural and ongoing part of the process of writing an essay.

Name ______________________ Date ______________

The Final Zing!

You can use this page to help you write a strong conclusion.

Thesis:

____

____

Summary of Main Points:

____

____

____

____

____

____

The Final Zing (Look in your notes for quotes, surprising facts, and so on):

____

____

____

____

Work on your conclusion on a separate sheet of paper. When you're satisfied, copy it below.

Your Conclusion:

____

____

____

____

____

____

____

____

Transitions

◆ Purpose ◆

To demonstrate how transitional words and phrases link the sentences and paragraphs in an essay

Although students may know how to develop an essay, their paragraphs often read and sound more like a list of sentences instead of a related group. Their paragraphs may stand solidly by themselves rather than leading logically from one to another. This lack of cohesiveness can confuse the reader, so it's important for students to understand the importance of using transitions, within paragraphs and between them.

Often, when students do include transitions, they use the wrong word or phrase; for example, they may use a word to emphasize an idea when they mean to conclude or summarize. And in their enthusiasm, students commonly overuse transitional words. With some gentle encouragement and guidance on your part, young writers can recognize how to use transitions more economically and effectively.

National Language Arts Standards:

- ▲ Uses strategies to draft and revise written work
- ▲ Writes expository compositions
- ▲ Establishes coherence within paragraphs

Overhead Transparency

- ◆ Transitions

Reproducible

- ◆ It's All in the Transition

▲ Launching Activity: Transitions (Overhead 10)

Before displaying the overhead, pass out copies of the reproducible, It's All in the Transition, (page 43) so that students can refer to the list of transitions during this activity.

"From Andrea to Wendy: How Hurricanes Get Their Names" makes an appearance again. The first two paragraphs, with transitions added, top the overhead. After reviewing the information about transitions on the overhead, read aloud and discuss the two revised paragraphs of the essay. Think aloud to find and identify the first transition: *The first transition I spot is in the second sentence of the second paragraph. That sentence begins with the words, In fact. The words tell me that the writer wants to emphasize this sentence. He or she is emphasizing a specific detail about when hurricanes were first named.*

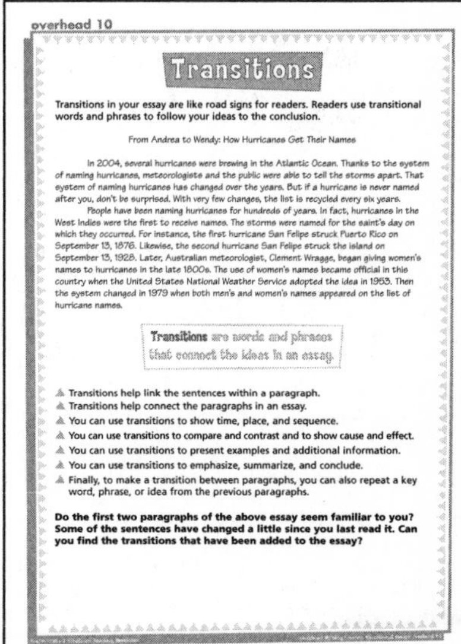

overhead 10

Transitions

Transitions in your essay are like road signs for readers. Readers use transitional words and phrases to follow your ideas to the conclusion.

From Andrea to Wendy: How Hurricanes Get Their Names

In 2004, several hurricanes were brewing in the Atlantic Ocean. Thanks to the system of naming hurricanes, meteorologists and the public were able to tell the storms apart. That system of naming hurricanes has changed over the years. But if a hurricane is never named after you, don't be surprised. With very few changes, the list is recycled every six years.

People have been naming hurricanes for hundreds of years. In fact, hurricanes in the West Indies were the first to receive names. The storms were named for the saint's day on which they occurred. For instance, the first hurricane San Felipe struck Puerto Rico on September 13, 1876. Likewise, the second hurricane San Felipe struck the island on September 13, 1928. Later, Australian meteorologist, Clement Wragge, began giving women's names to hurricanes in the late 1800s. The use of women's names became official in this country when the United States National Weather Service adopted the idea in 1953. Then the system changed in 1979 when both men's and women's names appeared on the list of hurricane names.

Transitions are words and phrases that connect the ideas in an essay.

- Transitions help link the sentences within a paragraph.
- Transitions help connect the paragraphs in an essay.
- You can use transitions to show time, place, and sequence.
- You can use transitions to compare and contrast and to show cause and effect.
- You can use transitions to present examples and additional information.
- You can use transitions to emphasize, summarize, and conclude.
- Finally, to make a transition between paragraphs, you can also repeat a key word, phrase, or idea from the previous paragraphs.

Do the first two paragraphs of the above essay seem familiar to you? Some of the sentences have changed a little since you last read it. Can you find the transitions that have been added to the essay?

Highlight the rest of the transitional words and phrases in the second paragraph as students locate and identify them. (fourth sentence: For instance, example; fifth sentence: Likewise, similarity; sixth sentence: Later, time or order; ninth sentence: Then, time or order). You may want to ask students to pull out their copies of the original essay (page 9) so they can compare and contrast the two paragraphs.

Finally, to emphasize the importance of carefully choosing transitions, substitute *In fact* in the second sentence with other transitions as follows:

Of course, hurricanes in the West Indies were the first to receive names. (Using the emphasis transition *of course* makes assumptions about what the reader knows.)

Therefore, hurricanes in the West Indies were the first to receive names. (Using the cause-and-effect transition *therefore* implies a prior relationship that doesn't exist.)

Student Reproducible

Distribute a copy of this reproducible for students to keep in their notebooks for reference. Also stash additional copies in your Writing Center.

It's All in the Transition: Encourage students to review their essays on working dogs and add transition words from the list. Also, challenge them to be on the lookout for transitional words and phrases as they read, and add the new transitions to this list.

Writing Practice

Have students reread their Writing Practice essays with a critical eye. Which transitional words and phrases should they incorporate into their essay to make the ideas connect and flow? Remind them to consider how the sentences within each paragraph are linked as well as how the paragraphs are connected.

Teaching Tip

When students write on a computer, they often have greater difficulty in keeping track of how all the parts of their essays are working together. They tend to lose sight of the whole as they scroll up or down. Encourage students to remember to check their transitions as part of their proofreading process. Remind them to always proofread a hard copy of their work, rather than checking it on the computer screen.

Name ______________________________ Date ______________

It's All in the Transition

Keep this list of transitional words and phrases handy as you write.

To Show Similarity

also, in the same way, like, likewise, similarly

To Contrast

although, but, however, in spite of, on the one hand … on the other hand, nevertheless, nonetheless, notwithstanding, in contrast, on the contrary, otherwise, still, yet

To Show Sequence/Order

first, second, third, next, then, finally

To Show Time

after, afterward, as soon as, at last, before, currently, during, earlier, immediately, later, meanwhile, now, recently, simultaneously, soon, subsequently, then, today, tomorrow

To Present an Example

for example, for instance, specifically, to illustrate

To Show Emphasis

again, even, for this reason, indeed, in fact, of course, to repeat, truly, with this in mind

To Show Place/Position

above, across, adjacent, below, beyond, down, here, in front, in back, nearby, outside, there, throughout

To Show Cause and Effect

accordingly, consequently, hence, so, therefore, thus

To Present Additional Support or Information

additionally, again, also, and, as well, besides, equally important, further, furthermore, in addition, moreover, then

To Present a Conclusion or Summary

as a result, finally, in a word, in brief, in conclusion, in the end, on the whole, thus, to conclude, to summarize, in sum, in summary

Editing and Proofreading

National Language Arts Standards:

- Writes expository compositions
- Uses strategies to edit and publish written work
- Evaluates own and others' writing

Reproducibles

- Essay Style and Format
- Proofreader's Marks
- Essay Checklist

◆ Purpose ◆

To emphasize the importance of editing and proofreading one's work

Writing an essay can be a long process. Once students have written the last word of their conclusions, they may feel their essays are finished. They often resist the idea of going over the material one more time. And it can be difficult for any writer to see what he or she actually has written. We often think that an idea appears on the page exactly as it appears in our minds when it doesn't. We need to encourage our students to take pride in their work. Editing and proofreading show that pride.

Launching Activity: Editing and Proofreading

Discuss the importance of editing and proofreading with students. They already may be knowledgeable about proofreader's marks, but it's always good to review the symbols and how to use them.

Tell them to ask themselves the following questions as they edit and proofread an essay:

- Does my essay have a title that grabs the reader's attention?
- Does my essay have a thesis?
- Is the thesis in the first paragraph?
- Does each paragraph in the body of my essay have a main idea?
- Do the details in each paragraph support the main idea?
- Does the entire body of my essay support the thesis?
- Does the conclusion wrap up my essay?
- Do transitions help connect the sentences within a paragraph? Do transitions help connect the paragraphs?
- Does my essay contain any unnecessary information?
- Are there any spelling or grammatical errors?

Student Reproducibles (Pages 46–48)

Distribute copies of these reproducibles for students to keep for reference. Also place extra copies in your Writing Center. To illustrate the information in these reproducibles, you may want to bring in samples of essays from previous classes. Use sticky notes to highlight examples of style and format in the essays. After going through these essays with students, place them in your Writing Center to serve as reference guides. Finally, have students use the reproducibles to proofread and edit their essays about working dogs.

Writing Practice

Allow plenty of time for students to edit and proofread their Writing Practice essay. You, rather than a family member or a friend, will be the designated reader for them. At this stage, it's important for your students to receive positive and effective feedback. You know how much they've struggled and how much they've learned. You know your students' strengths and weaknesses, and how best to address them. In a sense, this is graduation day for your students. After they edit and proofread their essays, they will have completed a short course in essay writing. You may even want to hold a "graduation" ceremony to celebrate their accomplishment!

Teaching Tip

Keep a supply of colored pencils—blue, purple, green, and red—in your Writing Center for students to use as they edit and proofread their work. Tell them that professional editors use colored pencils or pens to make changes when they edit. Also have pads of sticky notes available for students. They can jot down questions and stick the notes on the essay.

Name ______________________ Date ______________

Essay Style and Format

Underline the names of:

Books: Tuck Everlasting
Plays: The Lion King
Newspapers: Boston Globe
Television Shows: The Brothers Garcia
Movies: Shrek
Magazines: Scholastic News
Ballets and Operas: The Nutcracker
Paintings: Mona Lisa
Ships and Planes: Queen Mary

Use quotation marks with the names of:

Short Stories: "The Red Pony"
Chapter Titles: "The Industrial Age Begins"
Essays and Articles: "Berry Good Pie"
Poems: "Chicken Soup With Rice"
Episodes of Television Programs: "Lizzie Goes to New York"
Songs: "The Wheels on the Bus"
Lectures: "Three Easy Steps for Growing Roses"

Typing Rules

Double space an essay.
Use a one-inch margin on each side.
Don't use "fun" fonts in an essay.
Use a clear and readable font, such as Courier or Times New Roman, in 12 point.

The Title of an Essay

Underline the title of your essay.
Capitalize the first letter in the first and last words.
Capitalize all the important words in between.
Don't capitalize short articles and prepositions such as *a, the, in, for.*
The title should grab your reader's attention.
It should also fit the overall tone of your essay.

Names

The first reference to a person should use his or her full name.
After that, refer to the person by his or her last name.
Do not use titles such as Mr. and Mrs.
Follow this style:

> William Shakespeare would be pleased that his plays are still being performed today. In fact, if Shakespeare were still alive, he'd probably still be tinkering with *Romeo and Juliet*.

Name ______________________ Date ______________

Proofreader's Marks

Instruction	Proofreader's Mark	Correction
delete	the ~~cold and~~ freezing ice	the freezing ice
delete and close up space	the freezzing ice	the freezing ice
insert word(s)	last winter ^ in Maine	last winter in Maine
let it stand	our ~~summer~~ vacation	our summer vacation
spell out	(9) bluebirds (Sp)	nine bluebirds
new paragraph	"I did." "You did not." ¶	"I did." "You did not."
transpose	my friend best (Tr)	my best friend
insert space	Ring/the doorbell	Ring the doorbell
close up space	Who is it?	Who is it?
insert period	I am so tired ^ ⊙	I am so tired.
insert comma	coats shoes and pants	coats, shoes, and pants
insert quotation marks	Read the poem, Sand.	Read the poem, "Sand."
insert parentheses	Read "Sand" pages 10–12	Read "Sand" (pages 10–12)
uppercase	thanksgiving day (Cap)	Thanksgiving Day
lowercase	My Birthday (Lc)	my birthday

Name ______________________ Date ______________

Essay Checklist

Editing All Essays:

- ☐ Does the essay have a title?
- ☐ Are all the paragraphs indented?
- ☐ Is the thesis clear? Is it included in the first paragraph?
- ☐ Does each paragraph in the body of the essay have a main idea?
- ☐ Does each paragraph in the body contain at least two ideas that support the main idea?
- ☐ Do all the paragraphs in the body relate to the thesis?
- ☐ Have I used transition words to connect the ideas in the essay?
- ☐ Does the essay contain any unnecessary information?
- ☐ Does the conclusion wrap up the essay and tie in the thesis?

Editing Expository Essays:

- ☐ Does the essay present information about a topic?
- ☐ Have I researched the topic well enough?
- ☐ Does the essay contain facts that support the thesis?
- ☐ Are the facts presented in a logical order?

Editing Narrative Essays:

- ☐ Does the essay tell a story?
- ☐ Does the essay use the story to make a point?
- ☐ Is the material presented in sequence?

Editing Descriptive Essays:

- ☐ Does the essay paint a strong picture of a person, place, or thing?
- ☐ Have I used expressive language?
- ☐ Have I included sensory details?

Editing Persuasive Essays:

- ☐ Does the thesis contain a statement I want to prove?
- ☐ Have I researched the statement well enough?
- ☐ Does the essay contain facts to support the thesis?
- ☐ Have I used opinions instead of facts to try to prove the thesis?

Proofreading

Grammar, Spelling, Capitalization, and Punctuation:

- ☐ Have I checked the grammar?
- ☐ Are all the words in the essay spelled correctly?
- ☐ Have I capitalized all proper nouns and the beginning of sentences?
- ☐ Is the essay punctuated correctly?